environerd

environerd.com

Copyright © 2021 Katie Pelon

Paperback: 9798486512032

How to Use this Journal

Instructions

Bring this journal with you to the beach to complete fun activities and learn more about the animals living on the sand and in the waves!

Have fun!

Tools Needed

pen or pencil

sunscreen

weather-appropriate clothing and shoes

supervision from a parent or guardian

About Observation

Scientific observation involves collecting new information. Most information is collected in one or more of 3 formats:

DRAWING

You can draw, sketch, color, or paint, and add lots of details or keep it simple!

WRITING

Making notes using descriptive words is great, either in full sentences or not!

NUMBERS

Using numbers to note info about what you see is quick and easy!

Staying Safe

Use these tips to have a safe day at the beach!

watch the tides

stay with parents or guardians

never go in the water alone

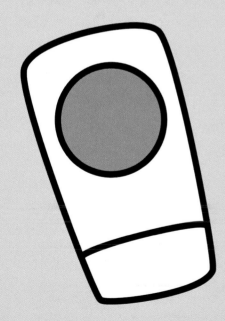

wear sunscreen

don't pick up animals

Recording Data

Noting information about your day before you start your observations helps you remember the day completely!

Weather (circle one)

Location

Is the beach crowded?

Who are you with today?

Date & Time

How far is this from home?

My Beach Day

Draw yourself and the people (or pets) joining you on your beach day in the space below!

Common

These seashells can often be found washed up on shore.

California mussel

speckled scallop

checkered periwinkle

Draw your own!

Seashells

It's important to leave shells on the beach for animals to use!

Draw your own!

sea urchin

sea star

sand dollar

Compare & Contrast

Find two seashells on the beach, draw them below, and observe their similarities and differences!

SHELL #1

SHELL #2

COMPARE: Things that are the same include...

_____

_____

_____

CONTRAST: Things that are different include...

_____

_____

_____

_____

Name the Animals

MARINE MAMMALS

These animals live off the coast and aren't usually seen on the beach. Test your animal knowledge and name their species!

_____

_____

_____

_____

If I Were a Whale

I would hear...

I would eat...

I would be friends with...

I would make sounds like...

I would feel like...

I would see...

Scavenger Hunt

Echinoderms are a group of animals named for their "spiny skin". They include the animals below. Find 3 of your own at the beach and draw them down below!

sea urchin shell

live sea urchin

sand dollar

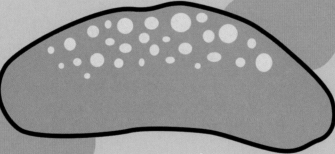

sea cucumber

sea star

The animals I found are...

1

2

3

Odd Anemone Out

One of these anemones doesn't have a partner.
Find and draw lines connecting matching anemones by
looking at their tentacles, and circle the one without a match!

Found Objects

What are these mysterious objects? Gather evidence and propose your ideas in the space below!

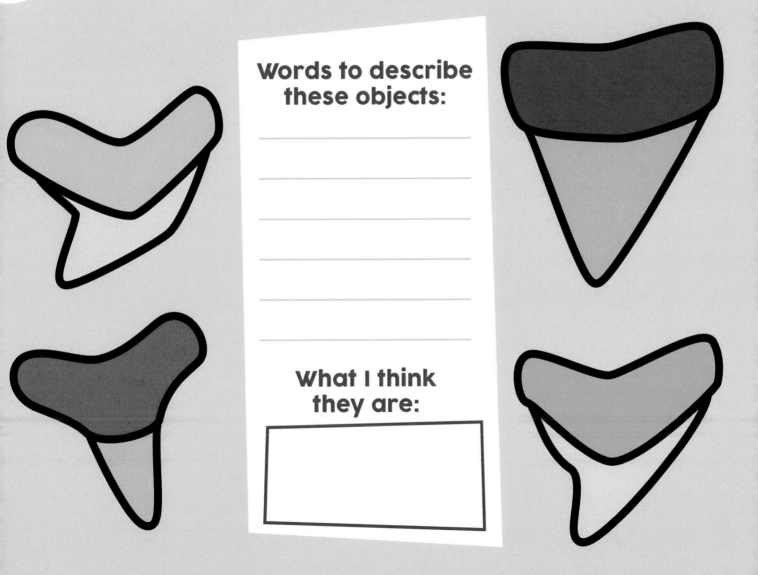

Words to describe these objects:

_____

_____

_____

_____

_____

_____

What I think they are:

Found Objects

We solved the mystery! The unknown objects are...

SHARK TEETH!

Clementine the Great White Shark has hundreds of teeth just like these. Practice drawing your own shark tooth in the zoomed-in bubble below!

Jelly Mystery

How does this jelly eat, swim, or catch its food? Share your ideas in the notes using your imagination!

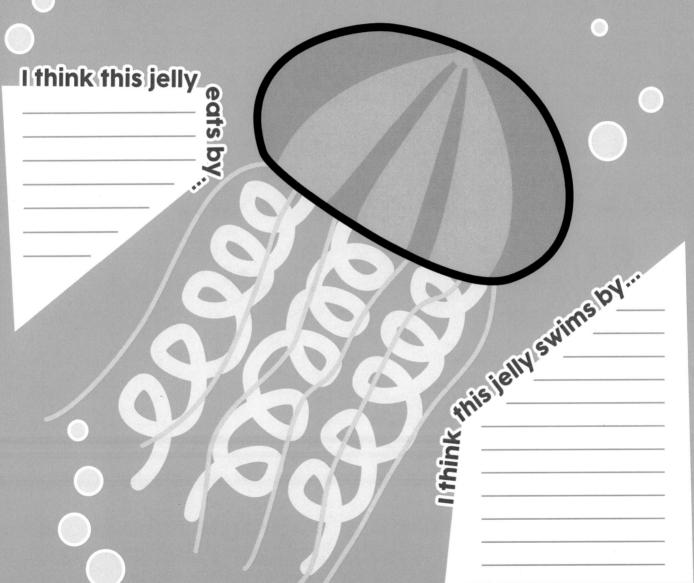

I think this jelly eats by...

_____
_____
_____
_____
_____
_____

I think this jelly swims by...

_____
_____
_____
_____
_____

Algae ID Guide

Marine algae, also known as seaweed, may look a lot like a plant, but it's actually not a plant at all! Algae is its own category of organism and is found in 3 varieties: green, brown, and red.

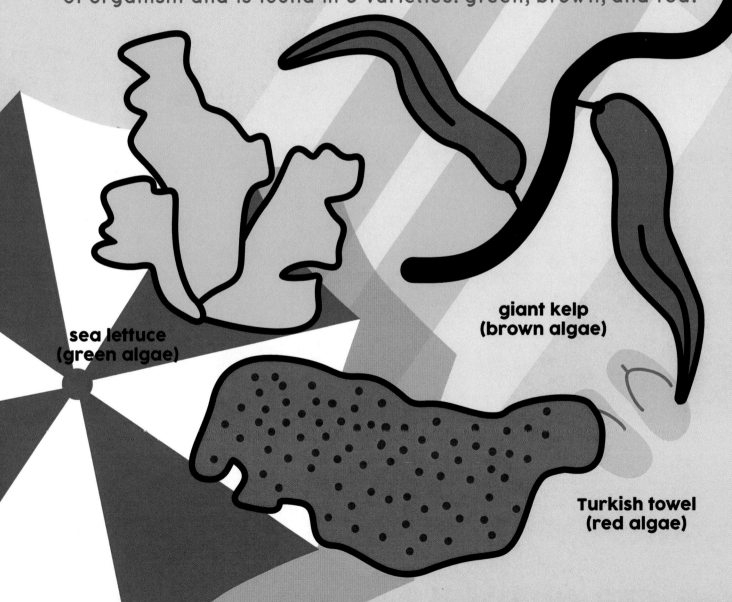

sea lettuce
(green algae)

giant kelp
(brown algae)

Turkish towel
(red algae)

Drawing Algae

You can often find many different kinds of algae washed up on the beach or floating in the waves. Find 3 pieces of algae on the sand and draw them in the boxes below!

A SLIMY PIECE OF ALGAE

A PRETTY PIECE OF ALGAE

A BIG PIECE OF ALGAE

Never Seen Before

Find something you've never seen before and record
your observations using all your senses below!

It sounds like...

My Object

It feels like...

It looks like...

It smells like...

I like it because...

Deep Sea Mystery

Bram the Vampire Squid lives in the deep, dark sea, and little is known about his species. Write down as many questions as you can about this mysterious creature!

Question #1

Question #2

Question #3

Question #4

Question #5

Question #6

Question #7

Scavenger Hunt

Crustaceans are a group of animals that include crabs, lobsters, shrimp, and barnacles. There are thousands of species of crustaceans in the world. Observe and note the differences between the 2 below!

hermit crab

shore crab

Differences between these include...

Color: _____

Shape: _____

Size: _____

Color: _____

Shape: _____

Size: _____

Hidden Urchins

Sailor the Sea Otter loves to eat food she finds in the kelp forest. Her favorite snack is sea urchins. Find and circle all of the hidden urchins to help her out!

Soundscape

Observe and record the sounds you hear all around you, starting with drawing yourself in the middle!

me

sounds near me

sounds far away

Name the Animals
FISH & INVERTEBRATES

These animals live in tide pools and in deeper water past the waves. Test your animal knowledge and name their species!

Beach Cleanups

Sometimes, you'll find pieces of trash on the beach, left behind by other people or carried to the coast from nearby towns by the rain. Here are some tips to help clean up the beach while staying safe in the process!

Recycling: glass, metal, some types of plastic

Trash: all other man-made objects

Use the correct receptacle

Wear gloves
Avoid sharp or dangerous objects

Use a bag or bucket
Collect what you are able to carry

Be careful
Stay with an adult at all times

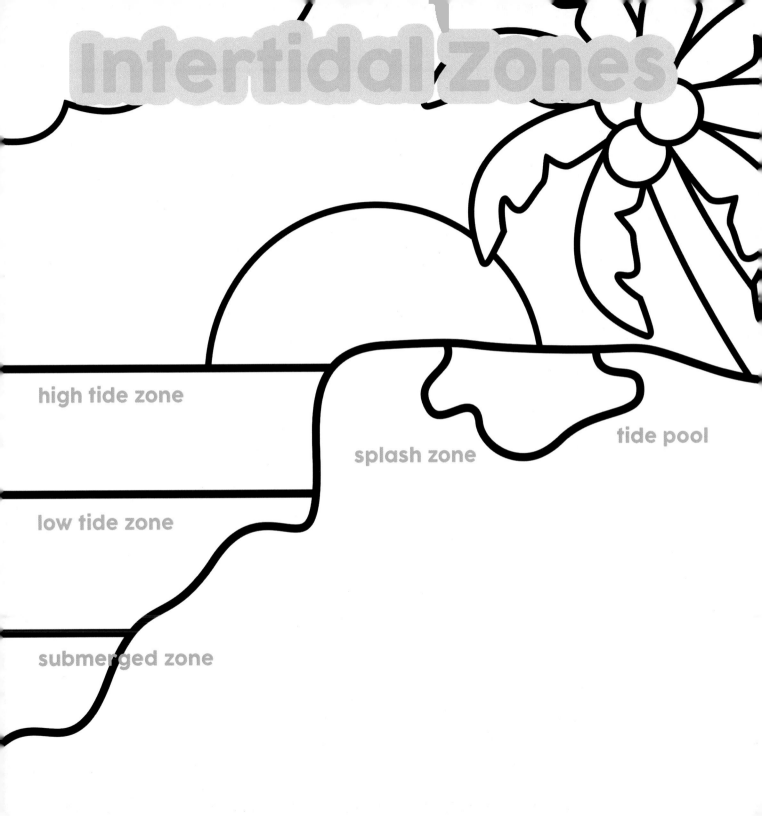

Intertidal zones

high tide zone

splash zone

tide pool

low tide zone

submerged zone

Reflections

It's the end of your fun beach day -
let's reflect on what you experienced!

**My favorite thing
from today**

**My least favorite
thing from today**

Mood (circle one)

**Would you like to come back to this beach?
Why or why not?**